T0071007

William Mathias

Shakespeare Songs

1.	Under the greenwood tree	page 1
2.	Full fathom five	5
3.	Lawn as white as driven snow	9
4.	Sigh no more, ladies	12
5.	Crabbed age and youth	16
6.	Dirge	21
7.	It was a lover and his lass	25
8.	Blow, blow, thou winter wind	32

Oxford University Press
Music Department, Great Clarendon Street, Oxford OX2 6DP

Commissioned by HTV Wales for the Cardiff Festival of Choirs, this work was first performed on 8 February 1979 at the Assembly Rooms, City Hall, Cardiff by The Dyfed Choir conducted by John Davies with the composer as pianist.

Duration 16 minutes

Copies of this vocal score are also on hire.

To John Davies and The Dyfed Choir

SHAKESPEARE SONGS

WILLIAM MATHIAS
(Opus 80)

1. Under the Greenwood Tree

(AS YOU LIKE IT)

*The piano part in small notes here and elsewhere is optional, and only intended to assist vocal pitching. These sections should preferably be omitted in performance.

© Oxford University Press 1980

Printed in Great Britain
OXFORD UNIVERSITY PRESS, MUSIC DEPARTMENT, GREAT CLARENDON STREET, OXFORD OX2 6DP

Photocopying this copyright material is ILLEGAL.

hi - ther, come hi - ther, come hither, come hither, come hi - ther: Here shall he see No
17
f
Ah
Come hi - ther, come hi - ther, come hither, come hi - ther: Here shall he see No
mf
f Ah
f
e - ne-my But win-ter, but win - ter, but win - ter and rough wea-ther.
22
ff
Ah But win-ter, but win - ter, but win - ter and rough wea-ther.
e - ne-my But win-ter, but win - ter, but win - ter and rough wea-ther.
ff
Ah But win - ter, but win - ter, but win - ter and rough wea-ther.
ff
27
f

33
f
2. Who doth am - bi - tion shun, And loves to live i' the sun,
ff
38
Seek - ing the food he eats, And pleas'd with what he gets,
mf
Ah
Ah
Seek - ing the food he eats, And pleas'd with what he gets, Come hi - ther, come
Ah
Ah
mf Come hi - ther,
mf
43
cresc.
f
hi - ther, come hi - ther, come hi - ther, come hi - ther, come
cresc.
f
come hi - ther, come hi - ther, come hi - ther, come hi - ther,
cresc.
f

47
hi - ther, come hi - ther, come hi - ther, come hi - ther:
Here shall he see No
come hi-ther, come hi - ther, come hi - ther, come hi - ther:
51
e - nemy But win - ter, but win-ter, but win-ter and rough wea-ther, but win - ter and rough
57
wea - ther, but win - ter and rough wea - ther. (er!)

2. Full Fathom Five

(THE TEMPEST)

*Some Altos may be added to this line if so desired.

15
S.
fade, But doth suf - fer a sea - change
A.
T.
B.
17
In - to some - thing rich and strange,
mf
mf
19
rich and strange, rich and
mp
mp

21
strange.
p
p
23
poco rit.
Tempo I (♩ = c. 60)
Hark! now I
mp
Sea - nymphs hour - ly ring his knell:
Hark! now I
mp
Sea - nymphs hour - ly ring his knell:
poco rit.
Tempo I (♩ = c. 60)
f
mf
mp
sempre con ped.
28
hear them, — ding - dong bell, ding - dong bell, ding - dong bell, ding - dong bell,
ding-dong bell, ding-dong bell, ding-dong bell, ding-dong
hear them, — ding - dong bell, ding - dong bell, ding - dong bell, ding - dong bell,
ding-dong bell, ding-dong bell, ding-dong bell, ding-dong

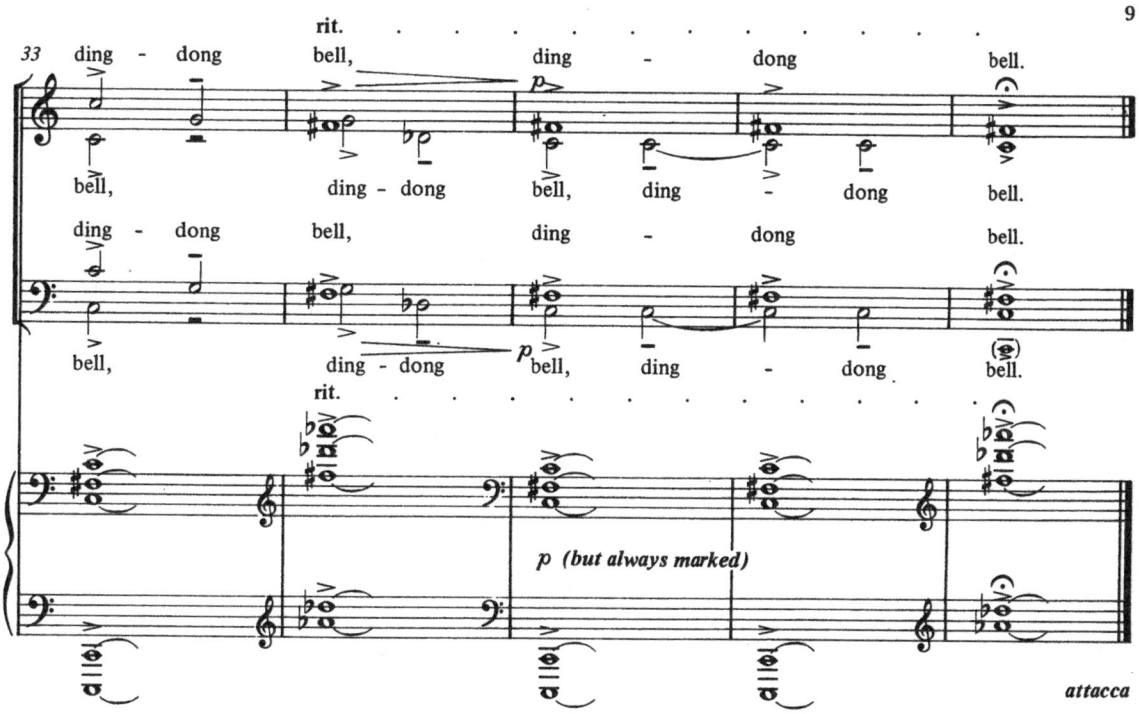

3. Lawn as White as Driven Snow

(THE WINTER'S TALE)

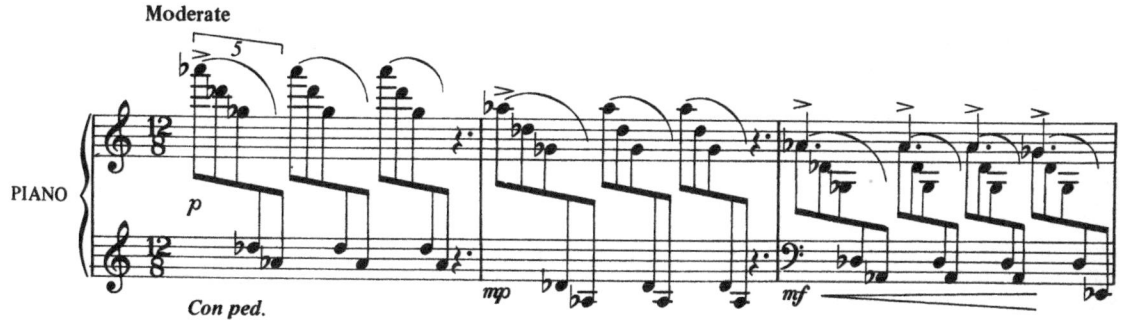

7
Gloves as sweet as dam - ask ros - es; Masks for fac - es and for nos - es;
BASSES
9
f (declamatory)
Bu - gle - brace - let, neck-lace - am - ber, Per - fume for a la - dy's cham-ber;
(f)
11
TENORS
f
Pins and
BASSES
Gold - en quoifs and sto - ma - chers, For my lads to give their dears, give their

13
pok-ing-sticks of steel; What maids lack from head to heel, from head to heel: Come
ff
dears, to give their dears, give their dears, to give their dears; Come
ff
ff
con ped.
15
(♪=♪)
buy of me, come buy of me, come buy, lads, or else your lass-es cry: Come buy of me, come
buy of me, come buy of me, come buy, lads, or else your lass-es cry: Come buy of me, come
(♪=♪)
19
(ff)
buy of me, come buy, lads, or else your lasses cry: Come buy!
(ff)
buy of me, come buy, lads, or else your lasses cry: Come buy!
fff
Ped.
attacca.

4. Sigh no more, Ladies

(MUCH ADO ABOUT NOTHING)

16
mp
bon - ny, Con - vert - ing all your sounds of woe In - to Hey non-ny, non-ny, Hey non-ny, non-ny
bon - ny, Con - vert - ing all your sounds of woe In - to Hey non-ny, non-ny, Hey non-ny, non-ny,
21
p
Hey non-ny, non-ny, non - ny.
Hey non-ny, non-ny, non - ny, non-ny.
26
Ah
2. Sing no more dit-ties, sing no moe Of dumps so dull and hea-vy; The

31
mf
Ah Then sigh not so, But
mf
fraud of men was ev-er so, Since sum - mer first was lea-vy. Then sigh not so, But
mf
36
mp
let them go, And be you blithe and bon-ny, Then sigh not so, But let them go, And
mp
let them go, And be you blithe and bon-ny, Then sigh not so, But let them go, And
mp
41
be you blithe and bon- ny, Con - vert - ing all your sounds of woe In - to
be you blithe and bon - ny, Con - vert - ing all your sounds of woe In - to

45
Ah Ah Ah Ah
f mf
Hey non-ny, non-ny, Hey non-ny, non-ny, Hey non-ny, non-ny, Hey non-ny, non-ny,
Hey non-ny, non-ny, Hey non-ny, non-ny, Hey non-ny, non-ny, Hey non-ny, non-ny,
49
mp p
Hey non-ny, non-ny, Hey non-ny non-ny, Hey non-ny, non-ny, non-ny,
Hey non-ny, non-ny, Hey non-ny, non-ny, Hey non-ny, non-ny, non - ny, non-ny,
53
rit.
pp
non-ny, non-ny, non-ny.
non - ny, non-ny, non - ny, non-ny, non-ny.
rit.

5. Crabbed Age and Youth

(THE PASSIONATE PILGRIM)

14
mf
Youth is nim-ble, nim-ble, nim-ble, nim-ble,
f
Youth is hot and bold,
mf
Youth is nim-ble, nim-ble, nim-ble, nim-ble,
f
Youth is hot and bold,
mf
age is lame, age is lame;
mf
age is lame, age is lame;
mf
f
19
f
Youth is wild, Youth is wild,
f
Youth is wild, Youth is wild,
f
age is weak and cold; and age is tame, and age is tame,
f
age is weak and cold; and age is tame, and age is tame,
f

25
Youth is wild, Age, I do ab - hor thee, youth, I do a -
Youth is wild, Age, I do ab - hor thee, youth, I do a -
and age is tame. Age, I do ab - hor thee, youth, I do a -
and age is tame. Age, I do ab - hor thee, youth, I do a -
ff
5
30
- dore thee; Age, I do ab - hor thee, youth, I do a - dore thee;
- dore thee; Age, I do ab - hor thee, youth, I do a - dore thee;
- dore thee; Age, I do ab - hor thee, youth, I do a - dore thee;
- dore thee; Age, I do ab - hor thee, youth, I do a - dore thee;
6
6

35
O! my love, my love is young: O! my love, my love is young:
O! my love, my love is young: O! my love, my love is young:
O! O! my love, my love is young: O! my love, my love is
O! O! my love, my love is young: O! my love, my love is
39
O! my love is young, is young, is young, is young: Age, I do de-
O! my love is young, is young, is young, is young: Age, I do de-
young, is young, is young, is young, is young: Age, I do de-
young, is young, is young, is young, is young: Age, I do de-
ff
ff
ff
ff

43
(a little quicker; playfully)
mf
- fy thee, de-fy thee, de - fy thee:
O! sweet shep-herd,
- fy thee, de-fy thee, de - fy thee:
- fy thee, de-fy thee, de - fy thee:
- fy thee, de-fy thee, de - fy thee:
(a little quicker; playfully)
f
ff
47
hie thee, For me-thinks thou stay'st too long.
6
6
8
6
mf
mp

6. Dirge

(CYMBELINE)

11
ALTOS
p
Fear no more the frown o' the great, Thou art past the tyrant's stroke: Care no more to clothe and eat; To
BASSES
p
p
14
SOPRANOS
mf
f
thee the reed is as the oak; The scep-tre, learn-ing, phy-sic, must All fol-low this, and come to
TENORS
mf
mf
f trem.
17
Quicker (♩ = ♩. 60)
S.
A.
f
f
dust.
Fear no more the light-ning - flash,
T.
B.
f
f
Quicker (♩ = ♩. 60)
9
f

19
Nor the all - dread-ed thunder - stone; Fear not slan - der, cen - sure rash;
21
Thou hast fin - ish'd joy and moan: All lov - ers young, all lov - ers must Con -
rit.
f
rit.
f trem.
Tempo I (♩ = c. 42)
23
- sign to thee, and come to dust. No
mf
mp
Tempo I (♩ = c. 42)
mf
mp

26
ex - or-ci - ser harm thee! Nor no witchcraft charm thee! Ghost un-laid for-bear thee!
mp
29
No-thing ill come near thee! Qui - et con - sum-ma-tion have; And re -
mp
mp
trem.
32
ALTOS
-nown-ed be thy grave!
p
pp
mf
mp
mp
attacca

7. It was a Lover and his Lass

(AS YOU LIKE IT)

† Only those adept at whistling. Alternatively, this part may be played by a group of recorders.

11
SOPRANOS
mp
mp
Sweet lov-ers love the spring.
ALTOS
mp
2. Be -
T./B.
mp
mp
mp
14
- tween the ac-res of the rye, With a hey, and a ho, and a hey no-ni- no, These pretty country folks would lie, In the
mf
mp
(sempre con ped.)
(sim.)

17
mf
spring time, the on- ly pret - ty ring time, When birds do sing, hey ding a ding, ding;
(whistling)
mf
mf
20
p
3. This
mp
Sweet lovers love the spring.
mp
mp
mp

23
carol they began that hour, With a hey, and a ho, and a hey no-ni - no, How that a life was but a flower In the
p
3. This carol they began that hour, With a hey, and a ho, and a hey no-ni - no, How that a life was but a
p
mp
p
26
mp
spring time, the on - ly pret - ty ring time, When birds do sing, hey ding a ding, ding;
mp
flower In the spring time, the on - ly pret - ty ring time, When birds do sing, hey ding a ding, ding;
(whistling)
mp
mp

29
p
mf
Sweet lovers love _ the spring.
4. And
Sweet lov-ers love _ the spring.
p
p
mp

32
there-fore take the pres-ent time, With a hey, and a ho, and a hey no - ni - no; For
mf
4. And there-fore take the pres-ent time, With a hey, and a ho, and a hey no - ni -
mf
mf

34
f
love is crown-èd with the prime In the spring time, the on - ly pret - ty
- no; For love is crown-èd with the prime In the spring time, the on - ly
f
f
f
36
ring time, When birds do sing, hey ding a ding, ding;
pret - ty ring time, When birds do sing, hey ding a ding, ding;
mf
mf

38
rit.
mp
p
Sweet lov - ers love the spring, sweet lov-ers love the
Sweet lov - ers love the spring, sweet lov-ers
mp
mp
rit.
mp
(rit.)
40
pp
spring, sweet lov - ers love the spring,
pp
love the spring, sweet lov-ers love the spring,
p
pp
(rit.)
p

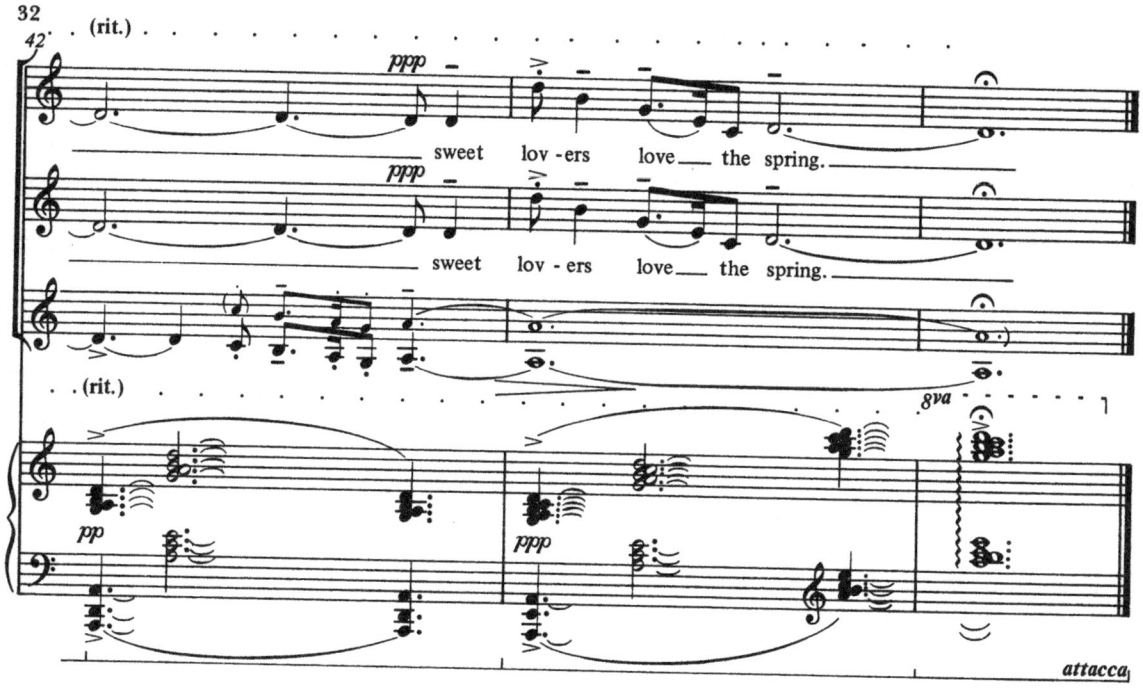

8. Blow, blow, thou Winter Wind

(AS YOU LIKE IT)

10
win - ter wind, Thou art not so un - kind As man's in - grat - i - tude;
13
Thy tooth is not so keen, Be -
mf
Thy tooth is not so
Thy tooth is not so keen, Be -
mf
Thy tooth is not so
f
mf
- cause thou art not seen, Al - though thy breath be rude.
15
f
keen, Be - cause thou art not seen, Al - though thy breath be
- cause thou art not seen, Al - though thy breath be rude.
keen, Be - cause thou art not seen, Al - though thy breath be

17
ff
f
rude.
Heigh - ho! sing, heigh - ho!
f
rude.
ff
f
ff
19
un - to the green hol - ly: Most friend - ship is feign - ing, most
21
lov - ing mere fol - ly. Then heigh - ho! the hol - ly!

23
This life is most jol - ly.
ff
27
32
ff
2. Freeze, freeze, thou bit - ter sky, That dost not bite so nigh As
ff
trem.
ff
Ped.

35
ben - e - fits for-got:
Though
mf
Though
mf
f
3
3
37
thou the wa-ters warp, Thy sting is not so sharp As
mf
Though thou the wa - ters warp, Thy sting is not so
thou the wa-ters warp, Thy sting is not so sharp As
mf
Though thou the wa - ters warp, Thy sting is not so
mf
friend re - mem - bered not.
39
f
sharp As friend re - mem-bered not.
f
friend re - mem.- bered not.
f
f
sharp As friend re - mem-bered not.
f

41
ff
Heigh - ho! sing, heigh - ho!
ff
ff
43
un - to the green hol - ly: Most friend - ship is feign - ing, most
45
lov - ing mere fol - ly. Then heigh - ho! the hol - ly!

Reproduced and printed by
Halstan & Co. Ltd., Amersham, Bucks., England